By the same author

Absence in Strange Countries, University of Queensland Press
The One True History, Hale & Iremonger

For *Absence in Strange Countries*

'McDonald brings to his poems imagination, a command of language and a sense of the bizarre.'
– Ludmilla K. Robinson, *Linq*

'*Absence in Strange Countries* is a thick, juicy, in parts tough, never overdone but often rare slab of life ... stagier but also more compelling than Larkin's "solving emptiness".'
– Christopher Pollnitz, *Southerly*

For *The One True History*

'McDonald is a poet for whom language is central ... and, I suspect, he issues a challenge to have fun.'
– Stephen J. Williams, *Australian Book Review*

'The King's English will never be the same. ... This is a monster of a book; difficult to put down, and difficult to take up again. A nervous energy propels each poem into surprising domains where language is both friend and foe.'
– Keith Russell, *Quadrant*

NIGHT MUSIC

Thanks to the editors of the following publications:

A Parachute of Blue (ed. Judith Beveridge), *Australian Poetry Journal, Best Australian Poems 2014* (ed. Geoff Page), *Best Australian Poems 2015* (Page), *The Bulletin, The Canberra Times, Extempore, Heat, Island, Loving Kindness* (ACU) *Meanjin, Neither Nuked nor Crucified* (ed. Christopher Pollnitz), *Poetica* (ABC Radio), *Quarterly Rag, The house is not quiet and the sea is not calm* (ed. Kit Kelen & Geoff Page), *The Sea's White Edge* (ed. Paul Kavanagh).

NIGHT MUSIC

ANDREW McDONALD

ARCADIA

First published 2017 by ARCADIA
the general books' imprint of
Australian Scholarly Publishing Pty Ltd
7 Lt Lothian St Nth, North Melbourne, Victoria 3051

tel 03 9329 6963 / *fax* 03 9329 5452
aspic@ozemail.com.au / www.scholarly.info

ISBN: 978-1-925588-43-9

Cover design Wayne Saunders

For the two of you

Contents

III

IV

I

These words

What I'm telling you now
is a ripple of air moving
at a known speed between us.
I keep my voice at a modest pitch
so as not to distort my meaning
or give unintended offence;
likewise I keep my distance
so as not to intrude or alarm.
After all, we hardly know each other.

Now you hold these words
at arm's length, so when they
finally reach you, you will respond –
hopefully not with that flat
aversion of the gaze by which you name
such a solecism as the one just made;
but, with luck lasting, by a slight
widening of the pupils, a shift in gaze
or the soft intake of breath that says,

Ah, so it's you; haven't we met before?

Drunken tears

She is saying something as the floor moves
and her feet shift against the tilt of drink.
The music moves them lightly as someone shoves
through, heading for the fridge and the kitchen sink.

"There's so much they don't want you to think,"
she says. The music rattles in its grooves,
his hearing blurs like water dripped on ink.
They hold discreetly, a courtesy of past loves

that crossed dark rooms to find the lights.
"There's so much I'm trying to say to you,"
she says, forgetting who he is. By rights

each should be abed with nothing more to do
than guard their thoughts and hold their tongue.
They keep moving while a song of sorts is sung.

That tree

It was a good time
it was a bad time.
Why?
This woman and
that tree.

It rained a lot.
The tree
had no roof.
Leaves did not
choke its gutters.

The gum with its
dying limbs
and the jacaranda
getting too big for its roots –
neither
is that tree.

Hate ivy
in all its forms.

Sometimes there was wind
and various crows.
They knew about
that tree.

Washaways show you
the under tree,
the tree you can't see.

The ludicrous notion
of possessions.
Wood from the tree
makes things I want
to hold.

Buddha sat
under one.
Jesus climbed up one.
No, not it,
not that tree.
Yggdrasil?
Uh-huh.

Lie down under the shade
of a tree.
Can't find the tree?
Look first for the shade:
tree's bound to be
somewhere round here.

The south wind blows.
Petals, seed fly through the air.
North wind's good too.

Judas, various strange fruit.   >

Notable slaughters.
The tree shrugs,
an innocent bystander.

Dead smell in the air.
You try to be hopeful
about spring. And the tree?
Miles from here.

Smooth as beech,
craggy as cottonwood.
Now you're talking,
the feel of that tree.

I'm itchy. Go on:
you scratch my bark
I'll scratch yours.

Foothold to handhold,
easy. Up you go.
First limb just
forty feet from the ground.

Look at it this way –
where would you be
without that tree?

Arrivals

Sydney could have been in San Francisco.
Drake made Cook's mistake and sailed past the Bay
in a fog, fetching up instead at bleak Bodega.
"Nothing of value to the Crown," he wrote, c. 1578,
turning the key on history and binding us
to sandstone, not sequoia. So we missed 200 years,
and thanks to Drake our bridge is humped
not golden, and the beaches a sight better.

For us, landfall is landglide, the plane
surfing a sea of red roofs and pools that blend
in a quick blip to harbour and pre-Mascot grey.
Nearing home – and look, the Memorial Park,
with its concrete paths obligingly cross-haired,
targets the innocent rusty-roofed house
of the bard of Leichhardt. Good day:
that's me waving as you fly in.

And I don't get how La Perouse failed so utterly
to peruse the shore to French advantage:
like the rest of us, he was winging it,
thinking he might drift through or stay on.
Years pass, and you find yourself rattling over
the Coathanger and thinking, "My town."

But think too of Tutuma, a landlord of sorts,
forty before he ran into whitefellas, at seventy

flying to Sydney for his first view of the sea,
pointing down and saying, "Look, stars"
(a constellation not seen in his country)

or think of dropping in from the west at sunrise,
the light aslant as you coast the air over paddocks
fleeced with drifts of mist.

Mistanka

Four o'clock: magpies stir,
murmur in the moonlit mist.
Frost clamps its cramped claw
on crisp quiet, chiselling
crystal in the bird bath.

Thalassa: Southern Tablelands

Half the state is flying east, spattering
everything that's still left to us with soil
shucked from the food for next year's bellies.
The speedo sits on a hundred & ten
and the air con is cool, switched on,
reassuring, like the dream of a lush future,
as the car guns to the lip of the bitumen wave
cresting into the next valley.
Flocks of cloud, silly as wheels, head
for greener pastures to scatter rain again
where it's welcome but not crucial: vertical
water, squinted after, denying, drummed
out of the dance – while what the heart bleeds for
is the horizontal: the clayed arteries
dry as a death rattle, damp sand no more
than gasping mirage, and the flecked blue
hangs, Japanese, and never breaks.

As we rip down the face of the hill,
towns crackle in greeting. Out here, tsunamis
tower a hundred red & yellow metres,
what's washed up has that whited coral look,
and being dumped is for keeps: the pearls
that were his eyes are gold, ingotted, globbed
from ancient rings, ancestral medals.
Wave-riding grandsons inquire about death,
their own. Sociopaths, knowledgeable in looting,

remind us how folk cling to the coast, sifting
pain and ashes; while here, where life also is,
we wade out through shallows of desire, grasses
foaming round our thighs, stepping out the un-
numbered ridges of the landlocked imagination:
cool, sweet, whispering, high and dry.

Memorial sightings

History does change, eventually,
like the lazy settling of dust
or fashions in photography.
Overseas visitors no longer stand
stiff as posts before the prized view;
they lean, stretch, leap, arms cranking,
slapping a grin on the embattled tank

careless of what it is, where it has been,
what mud it has churned, the bodies
falling under it, the shriek of metal.
Or they preen before the naval
five-inch gun: ooh, what a big one.
They are cheeky, naïve, happy
with where they have landed, in love
with the camera. One squints through the rangefinder,
the target takes to the air for his beloved, rejoicing

like the Taliban sniper at two thousand metres,
caught in Canadian cross-hairs.
The five-oh round snatches him, bursting upwards
in an explosion of shale and dust:
part of the debris he flies, rag and bone merely,
blown star-spread and tumbling against the blue,
a scrap, detritus, out of all proportion,
gutted by the laughter, the view.

They're rioting, or *plus ça change*

The news from Chad
is bad,
while in Mali
most would rather die than parley.
Diplomatic faces in New Caledonia
could hardly get much stonier
and the French, given half a chance,
will blow up anything for *la belle France*.
Life for the idle rich in Siberia
grows progressively drearier and drearier
as on the Russian Empire's chilly rim
things slowly slide from worse to grim.
For citizens and infidels alike, Kuwait
swelters in a state of hate;
across the border a million hotdogs broil,
salt fouls the drink, sand clogs the oil.
On autumn evenings the West Bank
ignites like a newly tanked-up tank.
Jingo blinds the Brits again, and Cameron
soon finds a podium to hammer on.
Down the Ganges drift remnants of the Raj
like slops heave-ho'd from a Thames barge,
as purring Gandhis cant and hold their own,
ready for the casting of the first stone.
Europe teeters, the crowd roars,
fanned to rage by financial whores.
As ever, in Tobruk

things are crook.

And in Australia?

Don't look now, or your nerve will fail ya.

Customs

Good evening, and welcome to our beautiful country.
At this point we must detain you briefly
for a few customary inquiries and inspections.
Your baggage and your shoes are to be left
in the places indicated by the yellow lines
while you step forward to account for why you are here.

We expect you to declare your intentions openly
and preferably in words of three syllables
(we commend *abjection, contrition, penitence*)
and please be aware that the guards you see around you
are fully armed for your comfort and protection.
You say you want to live in a country with no national song.
We encourage you to be candid with the authorities
at all times. Your photographs, discs and thumbsc... drives
are to be placed in the padded bag provided for your convenience.
Your memories will be downloaded for later access
by the authorised agencies and will be treated with due care
for your sensitivities. You may be assured of full respect
for all your ideals that conform to relevant statutes pertaining.

There will be a short delay at this point
to examine the entrails. You are permitted to watch,
should you so choose, but be advised that to utter a sound
will attract certain penalties. Any hope or other valuables
which you happen to have about your person
must be surrendered for scan and assessment and may

or may not be returned later at our absolute discretion.

Any questions you may have will be answered in due course

and in the appropriate format, rest assured. During this entire process

rest will be provided from time to time for you to catch your breath,

should any have escaped. Inadvertent groans will be scrupulously

redacted for the public good. Our aim is to meet your expectations

to the fullest of our predetermined ability.

We trust you enjoy your stay.

Conditions, needless to say, do apply

and you may apply, in due course,

to be returned to your original condition.

A prayer

after J.M. Couper

O Lord, in this hour of our need,
we pray you grant us your mercy
and visit your special favours upon us.

To the anxiety mongers,
send their worst fears, clothed in fire.
May their irons be left on and their gas blow out,
may their banks fail and their tanks run dry.
May it all be as bad as they feared,
only more so; grant this unto them, O God.

To the pedlars of paranoia,
send incubus and succubus
that they may truly know the malevolence
of heaven and earth; send Belial
to sever their thoughts from their bodies.

To the messengers of cant, the whisperers
of whinge and special pleading, the not-me brigade,
the I'm-so-worthy, it wasn't my fault,
to those who speak with chainsaws,
the if-only's and the his-faulters –
send a perfect blue bolt of thy wrath.

But to the quiet, the patient,
the I'll-try-harder-next-times,

those that pick up the pieces and carry on,
those who sometimes forget themselves –
from the coinpurse of thy bounty, Lord,
send clement weather and small hopes.
May it be ever thus. Amen.

Damage FX

for DT

In the mountains, it's a case now
of beer taste on a champagne budget.
The bracing air has the taste of wisdom
as your head clears to kung fu thudding.
What is the sound of one rib cracking?

The body leaves the soul by the mouth,
other choices being too constricted.
Poetry gets out too, hand over hand
down the ratlines, before it's too late.

Hoist sail over this misnomer,
plug in the jugular and let's make tea.
Court's convened in the stadium:
all rise for the tinkling crowd,
the roar of breaking glass.

Chorus 21

Literatuses – new generations looking into
art and its healthful evacuation of meaning. *Oomph!*
Understanding comes from reflection – no, from
rearview mirrors held up, as 'twere, to nature
interrogating topography, underwear, topsoil,
endometrium ... like fingers through layers moving

down into the non-existent heart, or thereabouts.
Underwear? Look, don't get personal and don't
get me wrong, *verstehst*? Try it this way: art as a sort of
grid, those stretched wires painters once held up to
a landscape the rapt mind would then amble over:
nature before and after the body actually arrives.

Ode: Marketown

JF, il miglior guida

It's shaping up as a day for reading cornflakes
packets in the supermarket considered as prolegomenon
to a proper reading of the *Purgatorio*.

Neon tubes flicker hendecasyllables
fitfully over your most obscure ambitions.
In the health food aisle, the pure products

of Australia go crazy, as the keep-fit generation
pumps iron for venery. Lacan's brooding spirit
(or is it the spirit of breakfasts past?)

is a presence even shoppers can't ignore,
while your poem shapes itself to a daydream
whose vision of itself your reading subtly denies.

Mock self-deprecation may equal praise,
but things heat up all the same. Down in the plaza
hot boppers rock their sox, but you're not

getting yours off to a drag artist razzing
tiny tots for cheers. What's the objective
correlative of fingers slammed in the car door?

Medicare provides the motive and its office
the stationery fitting for parking-lot haiku.
In a spotless car the voyeur's hot hand is soiled

with visions of stretch tracksuits and baby oil.
We're knackered for that. Would Marx like this?
Life as a handjob among the pressing throng.

At least here you can claim, "I did not
make this myself": that's your story and you stick to it.
The haruspex of cereals looks up to ask

Can Paradise be only four blocks away?

House music

A dubious music
suffering enchantment of the tongue
while the flesh walks.

As the sun blows in the trees
light slides into the room like an insinuation
and blusters round the roof.

The object escapes our bifocal vision,
but the subject is at home, crooning.
Hearing gleams and nothing rings false.

Forms: Fireman's lift

Your life is burning to the ground
but do not concern yourself.
Unruffle your plumage
because your goose is plucked;
soon you will be charred to a crisp.

This is the way of things,
so it is good.

Picking your way through the rubble,
look for what is left of yourself.
Squat – don't bend –
and work your shoulder
into the bowl of the pelvis.

Lift with your thighs,
holding firmly to femur and ulna;
get your clavicle nestled under
the ribcage, allowing the head to loll
below your scapula.
Take in the view from there,
the tacky inversions.

Orient yourself, then walk.
The way out is through the door.

Burning

Beyond all this
the wish to be alone,
simply here, without antecedent,
to have arrived
as if there were no plane,
no ghosts, no path.
From here
the view stretches indolently
burning into a distance without qualification.
Everything is to hand, everything
is gone: it is all one,
neither here nor there.
The light is kind
and admits nothing untoward.
Trees stand and wave, water runs
on the spot, rocks shimmer their electrons,
shadows flicker in the wind.
Yet the air's so still that its caress
is a mystery. The cliff
falls away at your feet;
all this space opens itself
like a first edition, just for you.
Pristine, without one soul.

Something about the horse

Northern Rivers Dreaming

The farmer comes home from the bank
after an argument with the manager.
In a thoughtful mood he crosses two paddocks
and hitches the horse to the plough.

The blade of the plough breaks open
the cool soil and hefts out the sod,
slicked and turned against the grumbled furrow.
He speaks to the horse's haunches softly
about this business; its thighs work up
a saddle-soap lather as he moves through
sweat and their scent. Before dark he'll cut in
a full tree's width of the rising field,
working across the fall, *boustrophedon*,
and leaving the plough like a bookmark
for tomorrow morning's start.

The grass turns to gold and his shadow
leans across two shires. Birds exult.
The river's a calm breast, a drowning width.
The bank manager should stop arguing with him:
it's a level-headed fellow who can find
space for one more wedge of beauty
in a falling day like this.

II

On birds

How hard birds work,
cleeking stalks to a stout trunk,
squabbling over their high stake

in roost and food, day and dark.
Beneath them, pale against dry bark,
hatched shells lie, a gaping scatter.

Two parrots, maybe for a lark,
peep the interval used by Bartok
(the fugue, solo violin sonata)

far up the branches' spindly ledger lines,
quite off the human page. Wings are a sign
heaving against air – remiges of light

stroking the sky's stunned blue bowl,
words that streak the hollow of my skull.

Of the invisible

If there were a dog in the picture
he might be pointing to what's missing here
with his curious or apprehensive sniffing
at what still stands just beside or behind you,
out of frame. Looking back, as though
from the eminence of a loved or yearned for
belvedere, we hope to see just what it meant,
that long cast of light down Glen Rothes,

and how it mattered that this particular view
included a small copse in the lower left
which only became visible after we had crossed
that treacherously pretty patch of boggy heather
(you remember?) – that, and the feel of those you love
standing by your side to admire this new
acquisition of the unobtainable.
Reduced to paper now, in truth

the one shot looks much like the other,
and the golden light that so moved you
is rendered simply as a small patch of dyes.
From this position, it is hard to be satisfied by
the aesthetic sense merely, or the composition
of all that's left out; trust rather to the fickle heart
to bring into the picture what we loved
but could not grasp or bring ourselves to say.

Barluack by Glen Rothes

Sing flat as loud as you like,
out here in the watery sun
on the slope of Barluack Hill.
The glen stretches away a few miles
and no matter how far you walk,
you can never enter it, any more
than you can step into any other picture.
Always you are on the edge, looking in
to what you never possessed, even
as you walked the length of it.
It's not the same when you get there;
it runs ahead like tomorrow, like the horizon.
You can no more take it in than drink the sea.

But your feelings, those you can own
as this music enters and ravishes you
from yourself: Debussy on earphones,
languid and voluptuous as any heavy-slung
heather-covered hill under the mild light
after tendrils of mist and flattened rain.
The land becomes thought as soon as you look,
emerging from myths of sword and cattle,
frost and Highlanders tough as the wind.
Look and sing; you have rewind, you have
memory and photos like a refrain.

Rowers, Derwent Water

What are the physics of this?
The footboard kicks back against your feet
as the water gouges into the oars
and the lake leaps under the long skiff:
something in this glowing wood pours
speed up your arms, and the propulsion's sweet
that drags us to the far shore.
So Newton saw it: as the poem writes the pen,
and as the photo I took more than thirty years ago
of my moustachio'd father at the oars on Como
directs my lens through Derwent's drizzle.
Siftings of water hang above the lake;
seated in the stern, I shield my camera,
cranking the frames through.

                    And memory,
how does it scull from Derwent to Como
and back, faster than 25 frames a second?
It's the private showing of a silent film
that runs while we swap places, taking turns
to knuckle down at the thwart. Green water
hisses its old song under the long hull.
The horizon heels over, just past your shoulders
as generations of rowers bend to the oars,
hauling in the flying keel from journeys
we've all made, will make. Time can never run
too slow. Upwards the ancient force flows,
from the feet to the arms to the dipping blades
as we head into the hint of a squall,
riding the long breakers into the Caribbean.

You

'Delphic' egg, was it, or 'Orphic'?
I forget, prophetically enough –
anyway, not one crowned with laurel,
newfangled ferns or such autochthonous
anodynes for a bowl of shelled feelings.

But mine are peeled, and here, to a vision
redeemed in the ellipse of your eye.
Orpheus never saw a lovelier world.
Wrung with tears, his head soared from the river,
never once thinking to look back.

Night

for Diana

Rocking the baby
I lull myself towards sleep on my feet:
more rolling than rocking,
this dulling dance with the basinette,
its rickety wheels working
a rut as recursive as fear or grief
into the floorboards.
As I say, guilt seizes the heart
tenderly, but as nagging as
the *nyah-nyah* of his knuckle-gnawing
in his wicker-work bower.

But it's not guilt, this time:
it's older, more primal, a terror
that clutches me without pity
as though the calm of his inaudible breaths,
the imperceptible puffing of bedclothes
silent against the whisper of the night rain,
simply beggared belief.
I lean over him long, feeling the small warmth
that rises with his milky breath,
the smell if not the sound of life.

So I can collapse back into the arms of sleep,
curled foetal until fear again
drags me dry-mouthed from bed

to out-stare the dark over him
sleeping like a babe.
Up and down, the vigil's kept till six
when the shriek and snarl of the day's
first jets, descending like harpies
for their portion of our life,
lead us safely to the realm of light.

Washing the apples

A cold rinse will not do
against this patina of wax,
nor buffing to a high shine
on a childish thigh.
Here is something altogether
more loving and more serious
that requires the power of soap.
The names tell it to us:
Sunlight, Preservene,
yellow cakes to keep us
in the light of health
and preserve us from darkness.
Not the darkness of sin,
for that worm in the bud
is here guaranteed excised.
Chemicals in Eden exact
(not exactly *felix culpa*, this)
vigilance over grubs
you loathe like poison.
So the globed fruit bobs
under your hands in a plastic bowl,
a world of death and faith.
To me, sceptic, the problem
seems more than skin deep,
not to be washed or wished away.
Yet I find myself still
doing your absent bidding,

saving myself in warm cloudy water
for a future opening like
an orcharded valley
drenched with light.

Forms: *Qi gong*

Knees off lock, weight sixty–forty.
To balance the yin and yang,
practise parting the waves.
It comes from within as you turn
your waist, the warmth of sunset
in your *dantien*. Shoulders relax.

Follow Fontane, who is moving
in the direction of the form.

Breathe. Pour *qi* from palm
to palm. As you move, your mind
stills. Move your mind still and
follow. Phoenix rises from ashes
of your desires. Empty
your desires and pour your mind
from palm to palm.

Follow Fontane in the direction
the form is moving.

White ape offers fruit, a swing
of the arms empties your heart.
Stop the flux of breath and blood.
Jade lady spreads flowers: stop
the flux of breath and blood,
the blur of mind.   >

38

Heart, beat and be still.

Follow Fontane
who is moving.

Practices, in 3/8

for D

I'm sunning myself on the splintered deck
and struggling once more with topology.
Indoors, you make huntsmen of your fingers
at Czerny's bidding: the clustered phrases
get re-, get re-, get repeated over and over,
taking the immense machine of Western music for a walk
until some kind of form flows, *a shape invariable*
under the deformities of times and practices.

The snails are into the passionfruit again,
out where we stooped for wild strawberries,
and the grandfather groans its atonal chimes.
I'm scribbling on the versos of 'zerotolerant organisms',
right side out as the frozen heart unclogs
or the *inside out* of systolic riffs thrumming –
the way Mozart's mechanic alighted in you
years gone: ignored, but canny as a homing pigeon.

The heart, I'll say it again, is a silly goose,
honking its tolerance of what takes us apart:
bent, stretched or shrunk by times and practices
but not, it says here, *torn or deformed.*
The hands, likewise, return miraculously
to a remembered shape, and after endless coaxing,
Mozart's fluid crystals or Chopin's sorrows
rise again somehow from a bed of tensioned wires.

Sea shanties, book 1

for Lewis

The sea's a breaker,
not much fussed
with matters of form –
snaps and sucks us
like crab claws.
Carapace and mush, body and soul.
You expected more?

Along here, several billion shells.
Maybe one in ten thousand perfect, unbroken.
Don't bother, stay where you are:
I have them.

Heading for the beach?
Apply sunblock,
bring Oversoul.

The sea's appetites
aren't necessarily
exorbitant:
anything big enough
to sink.

A figure recedes into seaspray
taking the waves, taking
the weather with him.   >

Between him and me,
spotless sand, footprint-free.

The seventh wave, they say,
or the ninth, the thirteenth …
Oh, come on!
The dumper's cracking its knuckles,
the whale heaves, just three breakers out.
The best-moated castle knows
what's creaming up to its walls.

The ocean's infamy
is bottomless.
Who, me? it asks.
Slave of the wind and moon.

Lifeguard? Here?
As much chance as riding the waves
on a skateboard.

On this coastline
five hard years back
a dozen haiku sank without trace,
mortal as flecked foam.
Car stolen: body image
swept far out to sea.

Montague Island, hull down
grey on grey, suddenly sunstruck,
breaks out a gleam of granite,
honey-coloured scaffold of sail.

In the rainforest

for Diana

I

Only a true naturalist (and just how natural can a human be?)
could plop cheerfully into the ooze primeval that reasserts itself
beyond the rotting duckboards which lose heart mere metres from the
                                                              camp;
but the adventurer in all of us, the he-person or impossible sheila,
quickens to the crump of a putative croc beneath the scum-flecked
                                                              waters
and that odd smack you hear, mingled with jungle cries,
is simply fear squashed bloodily on the necks of the intrepid.

Humans are a recent interpolation in all this dinosaur fodder.
Through the deflowered forest a path is blazed with orange nylon cord
threaded between symbiotic ferns and parasitic vines.
The track snakes past buttress roots propping up your love of the
                                                              ancient,
and fine fronds whose lash across your eyes is spiced
with a thousand barbs. Here the happy can find the red beech,
the eel-tailed catfish, the small tortoise paddling nowhere,
the coppery brush-tailed possum scratching in the crotch of a tree;
while the naturally crabbed can plunge into days
of thrashing about in thickets of a novel confusion.
In the rainforest, the footsore reader will see
what he wants to see – even what he came to see.
It is all written.

At sunset you put up flyscreens and prime the lamps;
your brain tunes to a low hum at the prospect of happy hour
and the jungle becomes briefly quiet. The light, already lifted
high into the canopy, recedes further; and from the grey stillness
emerges the figure of The Tropical, languid and sultry.
Suddenly the whole joint starts to creak and jive.

II

There's a suggestion that civilisation is slipping out of your grasp,
like the liana on which your despairing fingers lose their grip
as you're engulfed by quicksands. Tropical ulcers flare across your skin,
leeches get into your eyes, the jungle quivers and howls
and you might see, at a bend in the path, a skull on a stake.
By night, like Deborah Kerr in her tent awaiting the leopard
which it is no longer manly to shoot, you freeze,
hearing the fierce teeth of *Melomys cervinipes* gnawing into your pack.
Hurriedly you check your reference data on the mosaic-tailed rats

but on the night walk, trust your guide's impeccable American drawl
as he points out rare critters – like roaches, spiders, one sleeping bird –
and the thick, tempting but cruelly barbed vine, Tarzan's Curse.
You think of the swift and merciless running of the Pygmies
and their insidious ways of preparing White Hunter's Girl for the table.
Boomlay, boomlay, boomlay boom. Those drums are driving me crazy.

The rainforest is a maze in which you can get lost
within twenty paces: you've seen it often and should know better.
It is opportunist as all hell and grows furiously

in the crushing wet heat. Even where a track seems to run,
the sinuous and invisible snare of the wait-a-while palm
can lift a fourteen-stone man from his galloping horse.
It's a place that can choke the life out of you
and near tears with terror, you collapse gratefully into the punt
that carries you down the great, grey-green river which slices
like a sliver of glass through all this stifling green.
You should know the crocodile's jaws are a tourist trap
but when you see them you realise that what you most want
is for the beast to hurtle its huge mass into the water
and rush your fragile craft, those fabled jaws monstrously agape.

Self-portrait of the author, returning at dusk.
From within the gloomy and cavernous hut we look out
as he mounts the steps to the porch, blank-faced;
and behind him the dense growth, harbouring its indescribable
                                                            darkness.

III

From Daintree, the rainforest dollops down itself to the sea,
clumps of tumbled broccoli held back at the sand by an invisible
                                                            blade
before they topple into the reef. Hawking it on the surface of the
                                                            waves,
we're suspended above a stone jungle, a mockery of mere chlorophyll,
where a noisy darkness gives way to silence, clarity and light.
Here the creature memory dislodges one small grain: *native as a fish*.

Your camera can't pull the forest into its small room,

and the domestic ratios of your 6x4 prints lop the ambitions
of haughty trunks far below their clustering ferns and strangler figs.
Even the cinerama of your gaze can't seize the view;
the eyes, speculative as any land-grab, bring little intelligence to this
world.
It's a succession of screens, blind alleys, false exits; it lives
in layers the eyes can just focus to, sifting back through occupations
of space. There are no blanks to fill in, no ignorable ground
on which to fix the object of desire. Spotting possums at night,
you're fooled by the malevolent green gleam of the spider's eye,
the fattening water drop, the cool regard of stars piercing the leaves,
till your beam picks up the red answering eye-shine.
The eyes, greedy for life, bring little intelligence.
Hush, and listen.

It's not only what you hear, but what you don't:
past the thump of distant generators,
uphill from the shush of surf and the clatter of small creeks,
the sleep-rending cry of the scrub fowl, the cat-bird
like a jammed chainsaw: past these, there's the creak and snap
of trees moving, skitter and fluttering in the bushes,
the crash of some creature about its business, the groan of limbs
in wind, the constant motion
the stillness, the human quiet.
Listen.
You are the subject. Breathe.
A good poem, like a good forest, fills your lungs.

IV

Later, photos will show the vegetation as it always is –
clipped, still, dominant – and the one figure with her backpack
walking or standing, facing away or back, or paused
looking over her shoulder. The figure and the ground:
you, me, us here in this or that, this or another place,
leafy and green and trunky and bountiful and *there* as always;
and us walking through or standing in it, bodies dwarfed,
faces turned, presences here or there against a green ground.

On the human scale, among the litter and the understorey,
you feel the heat and light lifted from you, a burden or a grace,
winched, wrenched or clawed up into the canopy where it lives;
so at dusk, when the light dies and climbs into a peacock-blue heaven,
darkness does not fall, but rises like an exhalation from the ground,
a surrender, a signing off, a change of shift or key.

The trees assemble themselves in their lack of rows or thought,
higgledy-piggledy, overgrown with creepers and vines and palms,
undergrown with mantras of the unnamed, the undiscovered, the
                                        unsuspected –
yet all this vast hubbub has, somewhere or other, to stop:
at the sea, at the incision of a road, at the counter-text
of pasture or cane or tea or some other human blankness,
so that the voice of the forest must finally cut short
its ancient murmurings and chatterings, its breath steam up
the pane of some other idea, until it simply ceases.
From a distance, even a short one,
you look at it like a wall of something remembered,

ungovernable, unimaginable, but coming back to you and finally *here*:
you flash past in a car, or you get out to take a look,
you scan it carefully in a craning perspective or at arm's length,
you could almost hold it in your hand like a page.
The forest is illiterate, but it speaks.

III

And now

So what remains? The country loved by Yeats
bobs astern, and now – a meeting of minds,
aeons of hobnobbing with the truly great?

The night has its portents, clear signs
that as usual it's the mind that's running out.
The weakness of the flesh remains, repays in kind.

The dream has you waking with a strangled shout;
something burbles in a phlegmy grate.
It will pass; somehow you will wriggle out,

not really limber yet with a show of grace
that the body once embodied in its prime.
The house narrows, but not to that narrow space

you dreamed. The wicked song gets hummed, in time:
music for words, perhaps, and none too late.

Two exits & how to

1

You've been here forever, but it's as though you'd moved in
just yesterday. In the end, time has had enough.
The familiar slips its moorings and goes for a wander;
walking together, you hear a blurred rushing
that slowly resolves into the articulated tumble of water.
For you, the days here are eloquent and swift; they glint
and sing. Each day, the other grows sharper and closer
while you slip imperceptibly into your own blind spot,
an image fogging the retina, becoming a ghostly presence
to yourself. Where was I? each thinks, casting around,
and not quite sure whether oneself or the other will be first
to step through the kitchen door, out into the cool black
of night, that still night, and not quite make it back.

2

But it was hardly a quandary for you, poet, who always
resisted the pompous because omnipotent drive
for conclusion, the stickyfingeredness of it all, and cheerfully
gloomily played fast and footloose with the dark, toking its energies,
taking a hit-and-miss of the worn & spanking it to newness,
a world you could count on to stay exactly where you didn't put it:
till your broken-field running stumbled, toppling you abruptly
without even a look of surprise or a bon mot
into that same river once.

On hearing the first Akhmatova

Alive and foreign, it's a voice not yours.
Maybe the starkness of youth brings it on,
those bouts of silence, bouts of weeping,
like shadows falling on the sunstruck side
of ragged avenues of birch or fir;
or the sun crashing into the horizon,
gone in a flare of retinal red,
into a roaring solar darkness,
an immaculate degeneration,
the perpetual night of exiled hopes.

What is it with poetry and sorrow –
so painterly, romantic and consoling,
glaring with overexposure and migraine –
that turns us with longing towards your pain?
The bleakness creeping out of the heart,
the struck chill, the longed-for thaw far off
like the crackling quiet of old forests;
or the aching hands, the empty breath,
the discreet movement of the galaxies.

But perhaps the truer tale is more hidden, resistant:
just the blank of those long Russian nights
and history stealing into your own life,
publishing it to the glare of day and fate,
your mouth moving silently with spoken words.

The point, however

is to change it.
Swollen with sorrows, the music
sighs through the slow movement,
a lost soul, a shade, a wanderer
from another planet.
The earth chugs round on its axis,
intent, minding its own business.
On a narrow beach we camp and pray:
I feel a breeze *ich fühle Duft*
von anderen Planeten. The trenches
gurgle as they fill with blood
for the supper of the revenants.
A beach of stone by a freezing sea.
Rowlocks rust and seize,
the waters parch, the nibbling figures
sprawl in their trenches. Night fills
like a starved belly. At dawn
the *Trauermusik* drops, shifts round,
groans in its sleep. The shades
flare and murmur for their star.
Limbs are stiff and the engorged lips
smatter with speech. Crack joints,
rake hair, fold tents and go.

in memoriam Peter McDonald

Oh what a lovely

It was, in part perhaps, *una guerra
molto gentile*, a gentlemen's war.
Recall, said my father to a comrade:
in Alexandria Harbour, had not
the Italian frogman given fair warning?
"You should know, captain,
that I have attached a limpet mine
to your hull. You have ten minutes."
Not a scene from a movie
but a true story, and a life saver.

Twenty years later my father
(volunteer, hunter of frogmen) was primed
for me to take my turn at war. After all,
his enemy would later forgive him
 ("gone into the mists of the lost time")
for that slap under interrogation.
So it was manly, it was high time
for me to bite the bullet, to accept
the call and ship out to where
stoned troops fragged their officers
and shreds of human flesh
were hanging from the trees.

Window seat

As the hawk sees it, or the helmeted airman
or the passenger, long on fell chat, short on cash
with a comfortable bellyful of Bombay curry:
Stuttgart and Karlsruhe, flanking the Rhône
where the cars still run as visible specks
in the eye of the beholder, who sees it
as a bombardier might, 'with father's eye'
bombing prisoners clustered on roofs, on drives,
hurtling chemicals down upon chemicals,
the womb-seeking seeds of death unleashed,
given tersely near *Flugzeug* and *Schwarzwald*,
the land blackening from the parquet of faerie
to the opacity of history, lying below innocent cirrus
spread like a lover's hair in tendrils across
something black, brusque, pine-scented, like
fragrance mingled with sweat under helmet and scarf,
thinking of leman and *Hausfrau* waiting for seed
dispassionately bestowed among decelerating flak
that loops up towards passengers and flight attendants
as they fan out homewards over Mosel and Luxembourg
with tattered fuselage and brimming glasses,
sweet provinces to cool the imagination.

The middle period

With my first seven symphonies under my belt,
I can afford to feel ebullient. I retire for the summer
to my country villa at Vysoká, south of the capital,
and my eighth pours out of me in a fortnight.
I work at 'a rustic table of sawn logs' in the gazebo
with the heady scents of the garden and happiness
rising round me. My loyal housekeeper looks after me

and so does her daughter. Her skin is milk and nutmeg;
she has that lost, slightly surprised look
of the true redhead, very rare in these parts.
Every afternoon she brings me a foaming Pilsener
and other comforts. I notice that the beads of dew
glistening on the mug are counterpointed on her upper lip,
as I rejoice in a freshet of minims and crotchets.
She is innocent, and misses the pun; and true,

only the cognoscenti will understand the rising rhythms
of my new work. I conduct a public argument with my publisher,
the German pig, and win. My sales are rising,
the coming concert season is nearly fully booked already,
even Dolby's grandfather is passionate about my music.
This has been a glorious summer, my public adores me,
and it is only 1889. I still have fifteen years to go.

Forms: Vision

There is a leaf on your hand.
There is your hand under a leaf.
Your leaf lies on a hand,
under the air, under your gaze.
It is glossy, flossy, sprung
on the lines of a hand. The line
runs between the hand, your leaf;

without it you could see
neither hand nor leaf. The line
makes what it ends, what it
edges into or out of vision.
It calls in or cuts out, one
thing from another.

The line gives its lie to the eye;
the eye's lie is the line that says
this is the leaf, this is the hand.
Without leaf, there is no hand
and the winsome leaf needs a hand.

So: no hand, no leaf.

Voice

It nudges like a language you once knew
from a country you'd visited in dream
where the natives regularly gather
at some parliament, sing-along or mystery:
new wine and nibbles for the local deity
or a booze-up for the obsequies.

Farewell, it says between mouthfuls
in a voice you'd swear you recognised.
Come again? A sibilance turns your head
and realisation hits like a sockful of sand:
you're out like a light into old unknowing ...

Or it's like the pithy utterances of the dead,
matter-of-fact and loving, leaning
into a kind of acceptance of what
quite got away from them

forgiving all your foolishnesses,
your unpardonable grief.

Answers

The querent is here, with his large eyes.
He shuffles the pack of suggestions
like cold feet, and bites his lip. Cut
thrice, left-handed: left, left,
left behind the race, behind the veil
which we will now raise, if not rent-
free. He is his own significator,
an identical rhyme, a voice
silent in its motion. He lays
himself down gently, given up,
on green baize. Across his bird bones
and heavy heart is laid the first card.
This card covers him; others flank him,
their faces averted. There he is, riding off,
poling a punt; a woman is bound before swords,
a woman turns from him, he walks among rocks,
he lies on the ground pierced by words,
cups tip out their blessing under gaunt trees.
No Hanged Man, no Magician, no Fool,
no Queen consort with him. The auspices are ...
We wet our lips. He grows stiller,
turning to stone against the swords,
against what he has long known.

The way in

At times it can seem as if it had been there
all along, right at your fingertips, if only
you had been able to feel the texture of it:
the broad sweep of the bay like a wineglass or
a bosom of water, as you prefer, with the warmth
and languor of the lazy water and the natives
friendly as hucksters or Rastas, putting up
with your whiteness for the solid values of amity
and currency. That's unfair: the currency
is not so solid as we imagine, less solid than
this light which refuses to go out, and the view
it gives us of ourselves, slowly tanning
and achieving fluency, beautiful across the bay.
The sensation of suntan oil or liniment
is like a fragrant grit, encouraging complacency
and luxuriance. This could go on forever.
It's the kind of place we like to stretch out in
and not think about tomorrow, as though
we were still what we took ourselves to be.
The boats gybe like a bad conscience,
blotted out by the enormous glare. Jamming
your hat firmly down on your head is some help.

The fire of sunset takes a dive, finally,
giving the lie to things. The truth comes out
like white teeth in a black grin. *Tjibaou,*
tu nous menes à l'abattoir. The air

is sumptuous, but tanned at last we are lost
in the dark without that hint of a smile
that sets the mind running like an obedient fridge.
The nights are cool enough, once you get used to
the roar of the air conditioner. It beats sweating.
Some things are over as soon as they begin.

Exit

And the bearing for God,
how is that found?
What point of departure
defines the angle (oblique, doubtless)
that will carry a true line
out into that starred region?
"He left ... (dot dot dot)"
might carry the meaning, but not far.

Perhaps it would be like
stepping out of a room to find
the floor drop away suddenly
and becoming truly a bare forkèd creature
straddled over a joist or bearer –
or merely cursing in the dark,
barking up the wrong shin.

That's the problem,
the lack of the old certainties.
Drugs are not the fall-by they once were,
a shadow of their former strength.
Maybe it's like cooking or gardening, then:
that no one has merely half
an interest, lacking only the capacity.
No; with the proper care for oneself
it's something anyone can do,
with study, with application,

like the turn of a long wrist
mixing oil and tarragon for a salad
in the right season.

Listen up

Soul *ménière*,
filleted poet –
nothing much you could
get your teeth into,
but it does ring a bell
ting-ting, ting-ting, ting-ting, ting-ting
long enough to get on your nerves.

Eventually you twig: you're on
the menu. Push open the tall
baize doors and call out,
"Waiter, there's a soup in my fly!"
"What's it doing?" comes the reply,
"The mashed potato?"

So let me run this over you:
the mind's a contested space
like an intersection with no lights.
Send not to know – because you already
know the answer's a dead cert
and we've heard it all before, before, before.

These bones

Feet – what do they know,
nimbly looking for their sandals in the dark
while I slump on the edge of the bed,
going nowhere? These feet
bring me back from places
I never wanted to go to anyway;
they play blind arpeggios
among a clutter of parked shoes
while I'm numb from the knees up,
tingling from fingertips to scalp,
transported, gummy-mouthed and dumb.
After three hours' sleep, the whole corpse
is waiting for these feet to do their duty.

And why sandals? Because these bones,
moist metatarsals, like their curved bed too.
Feet, up and take me down that hall
again.

Walking in my body

Someone else is walking in my body,
clumping along, a canted swagger
rolling bow-legged out of shanty,
riot or mishap. He's fast enough,
but an ill fit to my mind's frame,
off the beeline of what suits my will.
This hobbled hobgoblin,
my hangdog scapegrace,
skulks inside me, slant-shouldered
scazon working against my grain.
Winnowed, flailed, I trudge on,
pride nipped by pain. In skewed circuit,
two strides before the sinew snaps,
I am walking in someone else's body.

At Kate's house

A hogget is a hogget is a hogget
by any other name, and that
is how it is at Kate's house. There is
the walking and the talking and the eating:
these are the three things at Kate's house,
and that is all.
        But first there is the arriving,
the sleeping on the train, the walking
down the Mall, looking at trees, buying
all the houses that are for sale.
There is the cooee at the door, the kissing,
then there is the talking and the talking
and the tea and the wine and the crackers
and then there is the walking, the bush
admiring and the talking and the tea.
Then there is the eating, and the eating
and the eating, and the more wine drinking,
and that is how it is at Kate's and that
is all. There is the hogget and the mint,
sauce for goose and gander, who are both
talking and talking and feeling and thinking
What will it be, the life? with all
the talking, the eating, and the sleeping,
the old maid of the mountains, the bachelor
of Leichhardt, in chaste beds
sleeping, and the walking and the talking.
That is all.

Oh yes – and the nose blowing
and the blowing and the blowing, all
through the walking and the talking
and the eating – nose blowing far into the night
in the separate beds sleeping, maid of mountains,
bachelor of Leichhardt, sleeping and blowing.

On completing another decade

This recessional could be worse,
given the body's years of sinning;
but how to make its characters reverse?
Say: hair paunchy, stomach thinning.

Sunday evening

Step outside into the sudden dusk.
The sun has melted into the earth, leaving
a throb of light like the reverb
of an unseen soprano, thin and high
in stone vaulting. The air coils,
with birds rummaging in the trees.

It is gone, this day you thought was yours
to hold; colours obscure as it rolls over,
turning its back on all your labours,
your certainty that this given day,
just this one, would hammer out eternity
fine as the sky's sheen of gold.

Never let night fall on a quarrel,
on lips pinched against kisses,
on a shut heart. At this hour life reels,
light is seeping from the sky, a sack
is drawn over the face of the world.
The finality of it takes your breath away.

Behind you, the house is unmoved
and the garden settles into its breathing.
The earth resigns its hold on you,
wheeling out into the far blackness.
The palaver of unseen birds blesses
your darkened head: let it never be worse.

IV

First man

for my son Lewis

Entering not as Adam, but as Adam
might have been: a youth, handsome,
buff in shorts, stirring up the audience
quite enough, thanks: their breath
ruffles the house like a sigh. His air
of innocence is both learned and true,
too good to be believed, headed for a fall:
you'd have to have been there and seen
the original. She, equal and accomplice,
leads in this: frank desire, a lust
to know – while he, innocent, thinking aloud,
casts the long last line that lands us at his feet.

(in *Paradise* by Simon Weaving)

Music in the foyer, Belvoir

for Sandy Evans

Old Himmler is here with his jailhouse crop
in the guise of a groovy guy, smiling
to let us know about that cool joint
stashed in his best bathmat jacket.
Signor Melisma scampers about, tickets
in his pocket, assurance on his lips –
but the rhythm section is taking it easy
(they've got it all taped)
and the bass, under his Mo hat,
is making an arco entry, quoting the Goldbergs

while out in front the pint-size tenor
in a monochrome Commedia outfit
stands under a glissando of frizzed hair,
embouchure emphatic, playing her heart out:
salsa's not too saucy for her,
nor the Trane from Alabama to Sofia, 11/8 time,
nor even Thelonious from Thessaloniki.
The backrow chatterers are at it, dahling,
gin and salt peanuts, but the listeners
are transported, dancing in stillness.
She weaves ahead, breathing with giant steps

till the tempo changes as we reach the bridge:
and there she goes, blowing her way
smoothly across it, showing us
What this love can do.

Charles Mingus knew my momma

Listen: you hear that beat?
The slapping of the sandals
on those big brown feet?
That's Charles.
d-bao, d-bao, d-baobao

You hear that finger
as it pulls the string?
the slap and sizzle that make it sing,
the way it booms, the way it sobs:
that's Mingus.

Third chorus, and you doubt my tale.
At Monterey he told the crowd,
"This one's for Duke – *I love you madly.*
I should do, I stole enough."

At Ronnie Scott's, the date mum's gift:
"Say hi to Charles," she'd asked,
so of course I did.
He nodded and smiled, arco mild:
"Sure, I know your mother,
she's a nice lady," the big man said.

Was the fire in his belly more belly than fire?
But the fingers were still alive alive-o
and what I say to you is no word of a liar:

the power of that sound could shatter smoke,
and behind it all was the drive of the bass
d-d-d-d-d-d-d-BAO, d-bao, d-baobao

(Alternate master go something like this:
horn players blew with lips he split,
she greeted her children without a kiss.)

You think what I say is outa place?
Maybe you think I'm right offa my face?
Oh no, uh-uh: *d-d-d-bao*
Charles Mingus knew my momma.

Her ain kind

Neighbours and strangers, we wave
as she leads a string of old dogs up the street,
while I slip through the fence to "the woods".
She'd take that misfit word, being a Scot.
Walking under trees in the even light
I imagine explaining to her why my name
sounds a wrong note in the mouth: "I'm a Sassenach,
but the line runs from my grandfather
back to Glencoe, or so my father claimed."

Mysteries of dialect and journeys swarm
as I chatter to her in my head.
On her leashes she tugs at an answer
simple as blood, weird as time.
My mother's sudden plummet
behind the hill of her mortality, now:
did she feel the veer and the vertigo of it
before the crab got its claws into her?

For thirty-two years
I've wondered. But it was there,
always there on paper and in my mind,
like much truth, hidden in plain sight.
Now from the Scots lilt it lunges for me,
a line from a letter my father wrote
in the year they dis-emigrated.
I want, she had said to him,

and she barely scraping sixty,
to die among my ain kind.

She told no one, of course, not even him.
But now at last I have sprung her,
the knowledge as crisp and clean
as the last of the malt whisky,
cool, golden and burning.

Cradle coda

Across the flattened darkness
comes a baby's squalling.
Someone comforts it, unseen.

How we loved him, blindly
holding his every cry to us.
Lost for words, we kept him close.

Lost among words, I try to see
myself, raddled and smaller,
as my last murmurs leave it all.

And whose arms then, as day
darkens, will hold me close
and deftly let me go?

Sea shanties, book 2

Land's the exception,
not the rule.
The summed coastlines of the globe
would take you to the moon
and back, three times.
Following the waterline
we leave before sunset.

The sea is steadfast:
never gives way
never backs down
never shuts up.

Two sails
on one small hull:
night black, blood red.
How did they know I was here?

Late afternoon sun
three-d's the tumbling foam.
Hold that
while I fetch a frame.

Pegged grey-mauve above the horizon
the cloud cliffs to a vertical Moby snout,
a flying mane of Ahab hair.

Forget the pool fence:
it's rough and tumble
slap and tickle
nip and tuck
twinge and twange.

Not exactly waving, either.
Putting a foot wrong
is not difficult.
The sea clears its throat:
it has a bone
to pick with me.

On the sand
we say we're *going in*;
up to our waists
we're *going out*, shivering,
but still heading for the horizon.

The lowering sun splashes
blinding gold onto the water.
Going deeper, I glance back
seeking his silhouette,
smudged but dancing in the shallows.

Paddling

A light breeze,
the water like hammered glass
dancing, getting ready
to jump out of its skin.

Cloud-carried,
the mind floats
depthless
all surface
above bottomless thoughts.

The water
will tell you nothing:
vagaries of light
gliding under your keel.

A watched fish
never jumps.

Look to the bank
for applause.
Only the slinking
parallax of trees
measures your passage,
the leaves clapping and waving
as you slip away.

The lake purses its lips
and huffs mildly,
letting you get away with it.
Out past the entrance,
the sea does its block,
won't have a bar of you.

As your shoulders
wince and fade,
discover a muscle
not previously logged:
extensor kayaki.

Wind at your back
can be harder work
than a headwind.
The prow lifts,
walking the waves,
stepping lightly in cloud.

Soft crunch of the keel
as you nose gently ashore.
Sit.   Breathe.   In good time
you will arrive.

All you need now
is one more life.

From the Flaggy Shore

for L and L, County Clare

Here history sits on the tip of your tongue
as the past walks quietly by your side
and everything that once was, still is.
The wind thumps and offers you a lift

to where the view is grand and mortal,
over the cliff edge to glide among currents
that hoist riding gulls and old memories
of what was and was not. Here the squat tower

watches the gusting sea, and we're all of us
soaked equally by the indifferent rain. Inland,
in from the Flaggy Shore, the turloch rises fast
from fissured limestone sunk below minding;

on the bothered water, unruffled swans ride out
the buffetings of what the weather sends.
Water is treachery, and water brings life
like bread to the worn table of memory.

Makar

for Lewis

This is just to say
that the website
I left on your monitor
is a window.
Open it:
it holds a poem.

Links spring
at a touch
bringing news
of how things are,
how we find them
make them, and be.

You are the makar,
so finders keepers.
The world is your
search engine,
succulent and sweet,
yours for the making.
Save and print.

Night music

1 Where are you now, Willie,
now that I need you?
Hiding behind the lank
hair of the moon?

2 The tongue stirs
in its embers,
an ashen coughing.
The dull root is thick
to know the mouth's roof.
Mouth, hello.

3 The door is open,
strange woods drip
at my open door.
The spade leans
against the toolshed door
where there are no shed,
no tools, no door.

4 Coming over the crest of the road,
looks like a dead cat, curled up
asleep, mindless of traffic.
Where are you, Willie,
while I face up to this animal.
It is a hank of hair,
someone left the top of his head

there for me. There: for me,
there was no need to go
that far. I look down gingerly,
tabbily, into the nylon part.

5   Car radio choir,
hum of the tyres,
boys in full voice:
German, the music
of declamation.
Zigzag of voices,
syncopation of traffic:
Christus! Auto! Straße!

6   The recorder speaks
of Heaven, it knows
that pitch of joy
beyond the moon's or
the streetlight's pale glare.
Smooth sheen of rosewood,
moist breath along the stops.
The fipple is sweet.
O for a tongue of wood
to get the tongue
between my teeth.

7   As I turn through the gate
the hair stirs, cocks
its ear, opens one eye.
No more, no less.   >

Gives cheek to all
and tongue to no man.

8   The words walk out on me,
smiling behind their hands,
so damn sure I'll come begging
for a thesaurus of mercy.
I hear dancing in the street,
a can-can of lascivious ideas
shaking its frilly lips.
Very well, if that's
how they want to play it:
a lock out. Bar the gates.
Good rid-
dance.

9   It's dead, that hair,
and it lies there
knowing its deadness.
Not bad,
not bad at all.
I take my
head off to you.

10   Cat, lick the bowl.
Cat, tongue up the
cream of my best thoughts.
Lap me, I'm thirsty;
sit on my knee.
Miaow. Pick my fleas.

Be the purr in my coffee.
Milk the next cow
in its lush green pasture.

11 The balloon's gone up.
Wait for the sky
to come down.
Umbrella,
sir?

12 Willie, you never answered,
damn you, the letters
I never sent. Hopeless man.
You'll be leaning against the door
watching a foxglove
and not thinking of me
in the slightest. That's
how it is, and how it is
with the high hawk watching you
and not thinking the slightest.

13 Sun's out, clouds move
leisurely. Trees breathe
in   out   in.   Listen.
Water is sliding over stone:
granite for you,
sandstone here, polishing
someone else's idea.

14   The door is locked,
        as if that were any use.
        The thief enters anyway
        and undoes my feet at the ankles.
        I am watching the print
        and as he lifts my scapula
        I turn another page
        under the pleasant lampshine.
        He leaves courteously,
        my mind tucked beneath his arm ...
        Willie, I have a bone to pick with you.

15   How can I cope with
        my own coping with
        the absent ghosts?
        There's a gap that haunts,
        and once saying is not
        enough. Sing it again
        and let's hear it one
        more time: oh yea, och aye,
        writing makes the phone ring.

16   Father Tongue is in his black box.
        Enter your half quietly, kneel,
        and without meeting his eye
        beg blessing. Confess
        how little you know.
        If lost for words, do not
        hang up. A silent contrition
        suffices. Father Tongue
        will then speak for you.

17　Cat sharpens the glint in her eye
　　while I slice liver with a dull knife.
　　Cat is a Manichee, black and white.
　　Cat purrs on my lap and knits,
　　ravelling up the knotted sleeve of care.
　　Cat is cruel, but cat is fair,
　　a yard of rug stretched on my floor.
　　I hum a tune that can't be sung;
　　Cat sniffs, then tiptoes out the door,
　　the door that is and isn't there.
　　Cat, come back; Cat's got my tongue.

18　Cock stretches himself,
　　demanding to be taken notice of.
　　He keeps a weather eye on things
　　but the dark is coming. He wants,
　　he wants, as usual, to be given his head.
　　He has a lot to say for himself
　　but I've heard it all before.
　　Cock speaks with forked tongue.

19　Willie, I had the blackest dream.
　　You weren't a strong, aloof,
　　cantankerous man, but a scared one,
　　weeping into lochs of whisky.
　　Write and tell me it
　　isn't true. Overhead,
　　the jets and curlews pass, if pass
　　they do. Try it now:
　　a light touch with simple steel.
　　See how your blue blood runs.

20   It's crabbed as a cabbage in here.
My lip's buttoned. I can still
thread a needle with my eyes
shut, but I can't make it flower.
The dark's got my tongue.
Water, just a thimbleful.
Help me grub my way out of this.

21   I meet you walking windy
above Loch Thom. The air is full
of words and promises
more rain. Meanwhile the sun
freckles the water like a trout,
the heather pretends it's salmon
and all that. We can see that
you'd be what a father
might be, and we can feel the sting
of the line between our fingers
and smell the bracken from here,
can't we.

22   The poem casts off
its glistening caul of silence
and slips out onto the starched
white sheet. Very good,
Sister Tongue, you may put
your implements away.
As the pen stitches me up,
I reach under my shirt
for a parched dug.
Here. Take this.

About the author

Andrew McDonald spent his early years in England and California and came to Australia to teach English. For ABC Radio he wrote freelance reviews and features; at SBS-TV he edited subtitles, then produced English narrations for foreign documentaries. He was active on the poetry scene in Sydney, claiming, with some justice, to be the bard of Leichhardt. In 2001 he moved to Canberra, where he has worked as a counsellor and editor. His previous books are *Absence in Strange Countries* and *The One True History*. Forthcoming are prose writings in *Glossary*, and poems in *And Now This*.

https://andrewmcdonaldpoet.wordpress.com/

Printed in Australia
AUOW01n1033120718
300090AU00001B/1